Let's Visit

Twelve Devotional Readings

GAIL GRITTS

ISBN -13: 979-8578463358

CONTENTS

INTRODUCTION

2020 has been a year of safely staying distanced from others, and sometimes loneliness has been our only companion. I invite you to grab a cup of tea, cuddle down in your favorite chair, and let's talk about the things we are feeling, the place we find ourselves, and remember God is still beside us. Let's visit.

Don't forget there are three previous devotionals.

Light that Shines talking about anxiety, worry, and fear.

Contentment and Captives addressing staying mentally strong and how to keep calm and carry on.

Build That Wall, which is twelve devotions based on my personal experience through depression.

You can access each video on YouTube at my channel – Gail Gritts. The chapter titles correspond with the video titles.

My weekly blog, *Beside the Well* is at
ggritts.blogspot.com

And, you can find out more about me at www.gailgritts.com

IMPOSSIBLE, DIFFICULT, DONE

Hudson Taylor wrote, "The work of God is in three stages, impossible, difficult, done."

When I first read the quote, I thought of ministry and life, the God of the impossible, and how the Lord brings us through. But today, as I come to share with you, my thoughts are different. I am still thinking, and no doubt, you are also, in terms of this virus and restriction. Let's take those three words and apply them to where we have been, where we are, and where we hope to arrive when this is all done.

Impossible – yes, we thought this was an impossible thing in so many ways. I remember starting to hear whispers of a lockdown back in January. But I thought, "That's impossible. How would that even work? Why would a government believe that was a wise course of action?

Yes, it might save lives, but what about the economic hit? Surely no government would take that risk.

And, possible – to stay in my house for weeks on end? To stay sane. To find some way to entertain myself for that long? To avoid becoming depressed?" Well, I guess we can all see how that has worked out.

We have faced the impossible, and most of us are alive to tell the tale. We haven't gone stark raving mad. We might be a little frustrated, but we're still calm enough to function most days.

And has it been difficult? I think that depends on your personal experience. If, like me, you have stayed cooped up and none of your immediate family have been affected, then difficult is better defined as inconvenient.

If you have lost a loved one, then difficult is an accurate description. I know of several who have not been able to be at the bedside of family members afflicted by the virus, who have not been able to attend funerals (myself included), and others who face losing their job.

Those who have been on the front line would say this has been difficult. And those at high risk or living alone have definitely faced increased difficulty.

I'm privileged to chat with colleagues worldwide through Zoom, and some of them are facing much more difficult times than me. Some serve in countries where people are starving, and yet, restrictions limit the help they can offer. Others are in countries where the government turns a blind eye, and they are helpless as they watch people dying.

Others face much tighter restrictions, even to the point of wondering who thought these things up. In one South American country, the government required a seven-day lockdown. People cannot go outside for anything – not even food. Why? Because they were not obeying the previous restrictions, and the virus was not under control.

It is a difficult time for every one of us.

If we are privileged to be in a calmer situation, let's not fail to pray for those who aren't. Christians are globalists. We have the world in our hearts, so let's remember to keep praying globally. God is at work. And our job at this time is prayer.

No one on the face of this planet has reached the time of Done yet. We are all in the difficult period. Done is many months away.

I find that hard to fathom, do you? I get to wanting to shake the rug and get on with life. Do you know what I mean? Just shake off the bad stuff and put things back in order. But it isn't that straightforward, I know.

And I think that's what makes this more difficult for me. I want a resolution. But God is the only one who can call time. My frustration is a sure sign that there is more for me to learn.

I need to learn more patience. But honestly, if I truly believe God is at work, even when I can't see it, I must wait patiently for His timing.

This principle of patience or waiting is throughout God's word. Isaiah 40:31, "They that wait shall renew their strength." Psalm 40:1, "I waited on the Lord, and he heard my cry." Isaiah even says, "the Lord waited." (Isaiah 30:18)

God knows waiting is hard for us, but He knows that patience does a work – "let patience have her perfect work," James 1 says. God is at work, even while we wait.

Patience isn't stubbornly pouting until things go your way or chomping at the bit. Patience is like working and walking alongside your Lord as He puts things into place – things where your hands have no business. Learning to let Him lead and knowing your time will come for activity, but it is His move right now.

I need to learn more about humility. I am catching myself spouting all sorts of hillbilly wisdom. Do you know what that is?

Hillbilly wisdom starts with, "Well if I…." It's the idea that you could sort things out if given a chance. To be honest, it is pride mixed with a lot of stupidity. If I ruled the world, it would be in a worse mess.

Humility means I know my place. If God had wanted me to be a part of the solution (other than prayer), he would have placed me with the responsibility.

What was it my friend said? "If God did not give me the opportunity, power, or responsibility to deal with an issue, I am to trust Him and pray for those who carry the responsibility." So, am I doing that? Am I faithfully praying for those who carry the responsibility?

Humility says, "There is a God in heaven, and I am not He!" I must stay in my place. Humility and patience go hand in hand, don't they?

And I need to learn more about listening.

I can't say what God is teaching you or whispering to your heart, but I am sure He is not silent. Sometimes, though, we aren't paying attention. We get side-tracked by the difficult situation. Or we get so focused on getting to the end of the trial that we forget this truth.

Spurgeon put it this way, "My soul, be thou in love with the way as well as the end, since thy Lord is the one as well as the other." I have this pinned up in my office. I need the reminder that God is at work every step along the way. I can get in such a hurry to get to the Done part that I fail to enjoy the process or learn the lessons along the way.

There is so much God wants to teach us and say to us during a trial that we would never hear or accept otherwise. But while we pout and stew stuck between our difficult rock and a hard place, we are not listening. We are busy complaining and whining. It would be much better to calm ourselves and open our ears, eyes, and hearts to what God is trying to say. He just might be shouting at us through this storm. Are we hearing him?

Let's finish today with a look at James 1:2-4. God's word reads, "My brethren, count it all joy when ye fall into divers temptations; knowing this, that the trying of your faith worketh patience. But let patience have her perfect work, that ye may be perfect and entire, wanting nothing." And there is the result – the done part of any trial. That we can be perfect, complete, and lacking nothing.

So, while we are in this difficult stage, let's be sure to remember that God is at work. He is doing work with purpose and for His glory. His work will produce a new strength in our hearts, a resolve to our purpose, and equip us for greater things when He says, "We're done!"

For thought:

Where has God proved Himself fully able in your life?
In what stage do you find yourself?
Where do you struggle to exhibit patience and humility?
What might God be trying to teach you through this trial?

Scriptures to consider:

2 Corinthians 2:14, Philippians 2:13, John 10:4, Romans 5:3-5

COVIDLY CONTENT

I feel very torn by this pandemic. On the one hand, I know I should be content, but on the other hand, I am frustrated with the restrictions and uncertainty. I understand the seriousness of our situation for those who may have a bad reaction to the virus, and it's hard to know why medical science keeps looking for a remedy when all my life I've been told you have to let a virus take its course. No one seems to know what is going on.

I am content – I'm happy enough, safe, and I know the Lord is watching over me. That's all I need. Still, I am discontent because I feel frustrated.

But if I am content, then I only need what God provides. Right? If God is with me, what else do I need? Even if I had an abundance of wealth or stuff, or whatever I might desire, and God wasn't in it, it wouldn't satisfy. Collecting stuff doesn't make me content. I'm actually finding less stuff is better. It makes for less to clean, less to store, and less to fret over.

I'm also finding when I take my focus off this pandemic, turn off the news, focus on something productive, and my relationship with God, contentment and calmness return. In that way, I morph the pandemic into something more useful, taking away some of the sting and frustration. When I try to exert my energy into doing what I need to do each day, even if it is only two or three basic things, I accomplished quite a bit instead of pining away at the loss of freedom.

I know the Lord moved my heart toward these devotional visits to help me keep my energy focused. Videos were not on my list of things to accomplish in 2020. But it seems to be His will, and so it now is mine.

Oswald Chambers wrote, "When God gives a vision, transact business on that line no matter the cost." I have that one pinned up in my office along with Proverbs 17:24, "Wisdom is before him, that hath understanding, but the eyes of a fool are in the ends of the earth."

That verse reminds me to concentrate, to focus on what I should be doing instead of looking around at everything else going on. I need to do what God has given me to do. That's always the best plan.

Let's visit a while about the idea of being more content.

To do that, we need to be living in and acknowledging God's blessings. They are there, even in this crazy year.

We have God's unfailing love working with our best interest at heart. The benefits of the Lord are free, purchased for us by Christ. And everything we have is from His hand, yet they are nothing compared to what awaits us in glory.

With every affliction or evil thing that happens, we still have the love and sweetness of God's mercy. It is renewed day by day – a never-ending supply – and all we have to do is ask. What a blessing.

We have a source of strength in Christ. We can do all things – right? We can bear our burden by tapping into His power.

Contentment allows us to enjoy everything we have because we know God is in it all. And whatever we don't have doesn't matter because God makes up the difference.

Lamentations 3:24-26 say, "The Lord is my portion, saith my soul; therefore will I hope in him. The Lord is good unto them that wait for him, to the soul that seeketh him. It is good that a man should both hope and quietly wait for the salvation of the Lord."

That's what we are doing, isn't it? Waiting for the salvation of the Lord? Not only for our move to heaven but also for this pandemic to be over – to see the end.

Contentment lives in our hearts. It isn't an outward thing. If it were, we would be satisfied with stuff, but you and I both know material things do not bring peace and happiness for very long. Only a relationship with Christ and His word alive in our hearts brings real joy and contentment – even when we are in lockdown.

Jeremiah Burroughs wrote a great book called The Rare Jewel of Christian Contentment. It is packed with gems of thought and insight into our malady of discontent and points the reader to truths and remedies. I liked this quote. "If he (the contented Christian) lacks melody in the world, he has a bird within him that sings the most melodious and delightful song."

Singing is a sign of a contented heart. Singing is a brilliant remedy for discontent, so raise rafters! Sing! Let your heart rejoice! Make that joyful noise!

How sad when we are not content. I think that is why we sometimes struggle with being housebound. Our home becomes more like a prison, and we look for any way out. The real problem isn't the house or the other people that are there. The issue is with us. We are discontent, and it shows when we are under pressure.

A Roman philosopher named Seneca back in 4BC said, "Those things that I suffer will be incredibly heavy when I cannot bear myself." He was right. Hard times seem more problematic when we can't bear ourselves. When we are discontent, we are unfit to accept difficulty graciously.

But God's grace is still there for us. Burroughs wrote, "Just as a child runs to his parents, so the gracious heart is carried to the God of covenant immediately where he finds ease and rest. If your heart works this way, it is an excellent sign of true grace."

Where do you run when things get tough or dangerous? That is a tell-tale sign as to where your heart is and where you look for strength. 2020 is but for a moment. It might seem long, but a thousand years is like one day with the Lord. We will survive. It will be worth it all in the end.

God is at work, even if we don't understand. Thankfully, we can open our hearts and let the Lord know how we feel. If we are content, we can shower Him with praise and singing. If we are discontent, we can tell Him all about it.

Just like Hannah. She prayed and wept before the Lord. The remarkable thing is, she didn't reveal her request to anyone else. She told God – that was enough.

After pouring out her heart and tears, 1 Samuel 1:18 reads, "And she said, Let thine handmaid find grace in thy sight. So the woman went her way, and did eat, and her countenance was no more sad."

Cheer up, friend! The same God who answered Hannah's prayer listens to you today. Tell Him all about it. Then, let your heart be content and your countenance no more sad.

Put discontentment away and replace it with the song of redeemed.

"Therefore the redeemed of the Lord shall return and come with singing unto Zion; and everlasting joy shall be upon their head: they shall obtain gladness and joy; And sorrow and mourning shall flee away." Isaiah 51:11

For thought:

What discontented thought plagues you?
How long would your list be if you counted your blessings?
Have you learned Hannah's secret in prayer? She prayed and went away with confidence.

Scriptures to consider:

Philippians 4:13, 19, Psalm 100:1-5, Ecclesiastes 2:24, 5:18. 1 Timothy 6:6

BREATH IN THE ATMOSPHERE

I have been so thankful for the beautiful weather we have enjoyed throughout nearly this entire time of the pandemic. In March, Tom and I were sitting on the deck and enjoying sunshine and songbirds. And sometimes ice cream. And, even now, we are doing the same. That is most unusual here in England. We've had a few days of rain and cold, but overall, it has been beautiful throughout. We have definitely had our intake of vitamin D and enjoyed breathing in the atmosphere.

The word atmosphere popped up in my devotional reading, and I have been meditating on it nearly all week. Let's visit today on some of the thoughts the Lord gave me, but first, let's look at the quote that prompted my meditation.

Oswald Chambers wrote: "The main thing about Christianity is not the work we do, but the relationship we maintain, and the atmosphere produced by that relationship. That is all God asks us to look after, and it is the one thing that is being constantly assailed."

I began by thinking about what type of atmosphere is produced by a right relationship with the Lord. My mind was taken to the verses mentioning a sweet-smelling savor.

2 Corinthians 2:14-16 speaks of savor – "Now thanks be unto God, which always causeth us to triumph in Christ and maketh manifest the savour of his knowledge by us in every place. For we are unto God a sweet savour of Christ."

The savor or atmosphere of Christ in our lives is a testimony to those around us. I remember a family who would visit the little country church where I grew up. They lived in Kansas City, I believe, but their kinfolks attended our church. When they came, they brought an atmosphere with them. As a child, I knew they were different, but I didn't know why until years later. They were servants of the Lord, full-time ministers of the gospel, and their fragrance, the fragrance of Christ, permeated the atmosphere when they entered our little sanctuary.

It made me wonder. Do I have the fragrance of Christ? Does my life have an atmosphere that blesses and brightens those around me? According to this verse, it should.

Another verse that came to mind was Ephesian 5:1, 2. "Be ye therefore followers of God, as dear children; And walk in love, as Christ also hath loved us, and hath given himself for us an offering and a sacrifice to God for a sweetsmelling savour."

The example of Christ is a sweet-smelling savor to God. And what is that example? It is the walk of love and the service of sacrifice.

Wow! As I thought about this one, I had to start questioning myself again. Do I walk in love? Am I willing to sacrifice for others? I think this time of being restricted to home might have pushed these ideas further than at other times. The atmosphere in our home depends on the walk of love and the willingness to sacrifice for others. What is the atmosphere in your home? Is it one of love or strain? Is it one of willingness or selfishness?

This idea of atmosphere is where I meditated most. And as I did, beautiful pictures flooded my mind.

There is the atmosphere of a wedding, the arrival of a new baby, an anniversary, and all sorts of life's events.

There is the atmosphere of nature, woodlands, the seaside, and mountains.

There is the atmosphere of the individual home created by those who live there.

Each church has its atmosphere created by the individuals of that particular body, and even nations have a distinct atmosphere.

But the sweetest atmosphere, no matter where we are on this planet, is experienced in our precious relationship and time with Christ.

Oswald Chambers is reminding us that this holy sweet-smelling atmosphere doesn't come from the work we do. Work just makes us tired. But the atmosphere that produces the most fruit is the one created by a consistent relationship with Christ. And that relationship is, as he says, "the one thing that is being constantly assailed."

Our enemy knows this truth. That is why he is forever busy distracting us, planting discontent in our hearts, and throwing every rock he can in our way. He wants to unsettle us. And sometimes, we too easily fall to his assault. The atmosphere in our homes begins to stink because we fail to forgive, grow impatient, get weary, or allow bitterness to take hold.

Our ministries or workplace becomes toxic because we lose perspective, become self-seeking or competitive, or fall out with a co-worker.

But here's the thing, the enemy cannot have free will if we are in the right relationship; if we are breathing in the right atmosphere.

Jeremiah Burroughs wrote: "When the heart of man has nothing to do but to be about creature comforts, every little thing troubles him; but when the heart is taken up with things of eternity, the things of life are of little comparison, he rises above the trivial distraction."

And that is the one thing God asks of us – to keep our heart focused, to rise above the distractions.

As Jude 20-21 says, "But ye, beloved, building up yourselves on your most holy faith, praying in the Holy Ghost, keep yourselves in the love of God, looking for the mercy of our Lord Jesus Christ unto eternal life."

We are to be in prayer, to spend time in praise, to meditate on the things of God, and feed our souls on the Word. Those are the things that create the beauty we desire and the atmosphere around us.

We cannot blame others or our situation for a bad atmosphere if we are not daily filling ourselves with His Spirit, if we are not putting on the armor of God and keeping ourselves in the love of God.

I'm finding, as 2020 continues forward, that the enemy constantly seeks to unsettle me. He feeds my moments of discontent and leaves me feeling flat, unloved, alone, and forgotten.

I have to remind myself that we are in a spiritual battle, and a worldwide health battle. Again, when I get my eyes off this pandemic and bring it all before the throne in prayer, God gives me a better perspective and a breath of fresh air.

I can let the enemy knock me down and leave me gasping, or I can rise above and breathe the atmosphere of heaven. I can let my hope drop in the dust, or I can place my hope in God and allow His truth and confidence to fill the atmosphere of my home and my soul. The choice is mine.

And the choice is yours, dear friend. The enemy wants to create a stink in your life. He is continually trying to knock you down and distract you from the relationship God has for you, but he has no power over the soul that is firmly planted in Christ and feeding on the Word.

Take time to evaluate the atmosphere around you – your home, your soul, your influence on others.

Work at memorizing Jude 20 and 21. Keep yourselves in the love of God and breathe in the atmosphere.

For thought:

Are you walking in love?
Are you exhibiting sacrificial service to others?
Do they smell the beauty of Christ coming from your life?

Scriptures to consider:

Proverbs 24:3,4, Proverbs 4:23, James 3:17, 18; Ephesians 4:1-3

TAKE CARE OF YOURSELF

In our last visit, I challenged you to memorize Jude 20 and 21. Let's read it again today, and then I want to share with you why this verse is so remarkable to me and valuable to you.

Jude 20 and 21 reads, "But ye, beloved, building up yourselves on your most holy faith, praying in the Holy Ghost, keep yourselves in the love of God, looking for the mercy of our Lord Jesus Christ unto eternal life."

This verse came alive to me several years ago as I faced the feeling of everything falling apart around me. I don't remember what events were happening, but I do remember when the instruction and comfort of these two verses gave me an anchor. And I know they still replay in my heart when I get that same feeling or need the encouragement they offer.

Let's start by taking this verse a section at a time.

Beloved – dear child of God, redeemed one, loved of God. I have a secure standing in Christ – covered by the blood, sealed for eternity. These two verses are written to me. And to you.

Building up yourselves on your most holy faith – building up. That tells me to keep building, my faith must grow, and the walls must be stable and secure. That will only happen as I apply myself to study and use of the Word. I go from strength to strength instead of sitting down and losing hope when I claim the promises and victories assured to me in Christ.

Praying in the Holy Ghost – oh, we could visit and visit on prayer. Prayer is vital to our relationship with God, for the strength we need to build, encouragement when facing uncertain times, the asking, seeking and knocking we must do. Praying always – spirit-filled prayer. Not just "Lord, help me" prayers, but ones that pray the promises of God, claim truth, and work with God.

Keep yourselves in the love of God. Now, this is the phrase God's Spirit rehearses in my mind. Keep yourselves in the love of God. No matter what anyone else is doing. No matter what is happening around you. No matter what foul attitude tempts you, keep yourself in the love of God.

To me, that says, "Gail, you have a responsibility to keep your place. You are one of the beloved. You have the love of God upon your life, so stay there. Do what it takes to participate in what God is doing in your life."

The word keep is significant. It means to have charge of; to guard, protect; to remain in a state of; to take care of, or to attend to carefully.

Isn't that beautiful? God is telling us to take care of ourselves, guard and protect, and remain in a state of—to keep ourselves in the love of God. We are not to walk away or let our position slip.

That is what I hear the Lord assuring me. I only have to answer for myself when I stand before God. He will only ask me about the one thing He gave me responsibility for – and that one thing is

ME! What did I do with the life He gave me?

Did I keep it safe?
Did I guard and protect my life?
Or did I throw it to the wolves?
Did I disregard my significance to Christ?
Did I tend carefully to my life – my health, my mental state, my faith, my prayer life, my service, and all of the things He has given into my care?

The last phrase – **looking for the mercy of our Lord Jesus Christ unto eternal life.** Am I looking for His coming? Am I ready?

1 John 2:28, "And now, little children, abide in him; that, when he shall appear, we may have confidence, and not be ashamed before him at his coming."

I don't want to be ashamed when I stand before him. How about you?

But I will be ashamed if I have not built my faith, maintained a spirit-filled prayer life, and cared for – or kept – myself in the love of God. Or, if like the foolish virgins, I am not looking for and ready for His coming.

Let's read those verses again, "But ye, beloved, building up yourselves on your most holy faith, praying in the Holy Ghost. Keep yourselves in the love of God, looking for the mercy of our Lord Jesus Christ unto eternal life."

That's a lot for us to do. Right? To be building, praying, keeping, and looking?

But let's not stop there. There is a beautiful promise just a few more verses along. Verse 24 seals the deal for me. **"Now unto him that is able to keep you from falling, and to present you faultless before the presence of his glory with exceeding joy."**

My heart rests here. There are days when I fail to build, when prayer seems flat, when my life falters, and I forget to look up, but He keeps me.

God is busy doing the protecting, the guarding, the keeping me in a state of. I am secure in His promise. Though I might falter, he will keep me from falling and prevent me faultless.

I know my faults. I see them, and the enemy loves to remind me of them. Doesn't he do the same thing to you?

But God has us covered. We are eternally secure in His promise. He will present us faultless before the throne with exceeding joy. And what a great day that will be!

Meanwhile, let's keep building, praying, keeping care of ourselves, and looking up.

"But ye, beloved, building up yourselves on your most holy faith, praying in the Holy Ghost. Keep yourselves in the love of God, looking for the mercy of our Lord Jesus Christ unto eternal life. Now unto him that is able to keep you from falling, and to present you faultless before the presence of his glory with exceeding joy."

And verse 25 reads, "To the only wise God our Saviour, be glory and majesty, dominion and power, both now and ever. Amen."

For thought:

Are you a good steward of the life God has given you?
In what areas do you need to practice better discipline?
Do you know rest in the love of God?

Scriptures to consider:

1 Thessalonians 5:18, 1 Corinthians 6:19, 20, 1 John 2:28

EXHAUSTED

This past week someone shared a list of eight warning signs of mental and emotional exhaustion. Another person put up a chart explaining anxiety, and the symptoms were similar. I had to laugh because so many are valid right now. Then, I thought, but do we pay attention to the warning signs our body gives us when we are under stress?

Sometimes we don't until we hit the wall, right? Until we say something unkind or lash out, we just think our stress is at a normal level. Well, no one's stress it at an average level right now. We are all dealing with something we have never experienced, and we may feel exhausted.

Let's look at some of these warning signals and see what we can learn and how we might help ourselves deal with mental and emotional stress.

The first warning signal of mental exhaustion is becoming too easily irritated. We hear ourselves complaining, giving short answers, lacking patience, and find ourselves in conflict with family and colleagues. Almost everything causes us to feel like snapping back. It all seems too hard, and we get frustrated with every simple annoyance or inconvenience.

Second, we might feel completely unmotivated – even to do things we usually enjoy. The things that kept us busy and sane a few weeks ago now are empty. We might find ourselves sitting around more, or watching more TV, or staying on social media for longer lengths of time. We just don't care now that the dishes aren't washed, the floors aren't swept, or the laundry isn't done because no one is coming to our house anyway.

Then, we might even be experiencing increased anxiety or panic attacks because the stress is building up. We focus our thoughts on what-if and if-only, causing our fear and worry to intensify. We can't concentrate on productive things because we feel restless and fearful, unable to control the intrusive thoughts that breed more anxiety.

Fourth, we might be having trouble sleeping. Or it might take us a long time to go to sleep. Or we might be waking up more often through the night. That is a sure sign our mind is not at rest!

The fifth warning signal is indigestion. Maybe you have a low-grade stomach ache or feel like there are butterflies in your stomach. This is nervous tension, isn't it? Stress works on our nerves, and since our body is inter-connected, stress will show up somewhere.

The sixth sign is that you cry unexpectedly. I know this one works on me. I can be just fine and then feel an overwhelming urge to cry.

And finally, we might feel detached from reality – just going through our day without responding emotionally or connecting to anything. We feel empty.

My first two videos were on anxiety because I knew for myself and my friends, lockdown would increase anxiety levels, and as the weeks and months have continued, those levels will have continued to rise.

I wish I could tell you there was an easy fix or a little pill you could take that would make all the anxiety and stress go away and give you back your emotional and mental strength, but I don't know of any.

I do know that if I allow my stress to control me, I will continue in a downward spiral. If, however, on the other hand, I place my faith in God's word, I look for the promises I need, practice my faith in everyday life, and keep myself in the love of God. He will carry me through.

Let's look at a few scriptures and some common sense to help us rest and regain our equilibrium and address these symptoms.

If we feel irritable – I find it best to get alone, give myself a good talking to, take a nap, drink water, or eat something. Maybe even indulge in some caffeine in the form of coffee or chocolate, and the irritability usually goes away.

To maintain motivation, we might even have to revert to a chart – a tick chart showing things to do and what we accomplished. I've had to do that through the lockdown. I make a note on my calendar and in my journal of what I accomplished each day.

Like I've said before, sometimes it is as simple as mowing the lawn or doing the laundry, but I have tried to keep moving quietly forward by doing something each day. No big splash – just a gentle paddle, but it all adds up.

People face anxiety, even when there is no pressure. The enemy loves to create paper tigers – imaginary threats, but that brings us back to 2 Corinthians 10:5 – bringing every thought captive and practicing the "wills" of Scripture and facing the N's of the Night by the use of Open Exposure and the Blood of Christ.

If this is your nemesis, you might want to go to YouTube and listen to the first two video lessons on anxiety and the two on the N's of the Night. Or, order the other three devotional books where you will find more on dealing with anxiety. Learning to control your thought life is a powerful tool for anxious emotions.

And sleep? Well, make sure you are good and tired before you go to bed. I find that even ten minutes of good exercise at bedtime relaxes my body and mind, helping me to get to sleep and stay asleep longer. Make sure the room is quiet, dark, and not too warm. Even simple things like washing your feet before you go to bed, using lavender scents, or gentle music helps.

For me, I remind myself each night is that this day is complete. I cannot do anything more or change it. Tomorrow is another day. Overnight, I can do nothing. But God is at work, watching over me – He slumbers not nor sleeps, right? (Psalm 121:4) He gives His beloved sleep. (Psalm 127:2)

So, I lay back and rest, confident that He will have a new day for me tomorrow, and I want to face it recharged. If there are things on my to-do list for the next day, I write them down before I go to bed, so my mind isn't trying to remember them all night. Power naps help, too. We do push our bodies too hard. I'm very guilty there.

God knows we need rest; maybe we need to be listening to the warning signals? I'm learning He uses them to remind me to slow down.

The body's reaction to stress comes out in many ways; indigestion is one we mentioned. I'm not a super health food freak, but I avoid all processed foods, even what my kids call plastic cheese. And I try to eat whole foods as much as possible. I have learned this over the years because my body has a bad reaction to chemicals, and I have found stress increases digestive problems.

There are other types of physical responses to stress to watch out for – holding yourself/muscles tightly, headaches, grimacing, or holding your lips tight. Stress has to come out – our bodies will react, so we need to listen, watch, and find healthy and safe ways to release tension before it causes a breakdown in our health.

Crying is another physical reaction. The best thing I have found is to go ahead and cry.

When I feel like this, it is time to go to God in prayer and cry on purpose. No holding it back, just letting it all out. God says He puts my tears in a bottle. (Psalms 56:8) That tells me He expects me to have times of crying.

The whole creation groans, waiting for the Lord's return, right? So why wouldn't His children cry about the sinful world in which we dwell? (Romans 8:22, 23)

Cry, lament, and get it over with. I've found I feel much better after a good cry.

And, finally, that detached, empty feeling. Oh, how the enemy would love to keep us there. But it is such a falsehood. We are not detached. We are loved, engrafted, adopted, made whole, covered by His blood, a part of the body of Christ.

And empty? We can only be empty when we forget that God's Spirit dwells within us, prays for us, and is ready to fill us with His love and comfort.

We must keep ourselves attached and abiding in the vine for the supply we need. (John 15:4) There is honey in the rock, dear friend. (Psalm 81:16) As the dear panteth for the water, so my soul longs after you. (Psalm 42:1) He is the water of life – draw from the well that never runs dry. (John 4:14)

Don't let the enemy beat you up with this lie. God is right beside you all the way, and His word assures you of His presence. There is no need to be detached or empty.

If you are growing weary and exhausted in the process of this pandemic, be sure to listen to the warning signals. Draw aside and rest. Rejuvenate. Then, take up your cross and follow gently on.

For thought:

What creates the majority of your stress?
What warning signals are you experiencing, if any?
What are you doing with negative emotions?

Scriptures to consider:

2 Corinthians 10:3-5, James 4:6-10, Matthew 11:28-30

STUCK IN A CORNER

Have you ever been between a rock and a hard place? Maybe life has pushed you into a corner, and you can't see the way out?

I've been there a few times. Sometimes the enemy walked right in and tried to take everything away. Other times the ministry needs looked daunting and impossible to navigate. But I've seen God change things so quickly, as easy as turning a page to start reading a new chapter. And there have been other times when I felt I would never get out of the corner, like God had forgotten me, and I was wasting away.

I was reminded of these times as I read a devotion last week from Springs in the Valley. The writer grabbed my attention with the first sentence—"It matters not how great the scheme if God draws it out." God draws it out. 2020 is being drawn out, isn't it? And 2021 will probably be another long year.

The writer goes on to say, "It matters not how insurmountable the difficulties if God undertakes the responsibility." If God undertakes the responsibility?

As I thought about this, I realized God is responsible. Not in the idea of blame, but the fact of control. He knows what is happening and how to turn the page. He hasn't left me wasting away in a corner.

Psalm 119:71 came to my mind. "It is good for me that I have been afflicted; that I might learn thy statutes. "

It is a good thing to be put in a corner? To be pushed and hemmed in on every side? My devotion reads, "until you are forced to stand with your back to the walls, facing a foe at every angle, with barely standing room." Really? It is good? Yes. Comfortable, desired, appreciated, maybe not, but good? Yes!

Why? Because in the corner, we learn to cast ourselves on God as King and Father. He works to lead us out of trouble safely. We experience praise and humility, and we encounter His faithfulness and power.

And we learn we are not alone. There is another in the corner— the Son of God walking with us through the fiery furnace. Sometimes, when you find yourself stuck in a corner, you find out what a wondrous Friend He truly is.

Tight corners create magnificent acoustics. Just think about how the Psalms of David pulse and reverberate the sweetest melodies. Can't you hear the verses of praise and deliverance ringing from a soul who knew hard times and challenging corners?

Tom and I have faced a few of these times, and one comes to mind I want to share with you. In 1995, we went home to the US for furlough because our support level had dropped too low. We'd just purchased our first building here in England and began carrying more cost, so we urgently needed to raise extra support.

We spent fifteen months home, and Tom was constantly on the

road, presenting the need from church to church. I travelled with him most of the time. Our oldest daughter, Sally, came off campus to live at home and watch the rest of the kids, who were all aged 11-16 – crazy times!

My health was not good. That's when I discovered IBS was my problem. Stress and processed foods meant I was in pain more often than not. We barely had enough funds to feed the crew and lived on the love offerings, but those few months – in a corner – still sing out to me! You see, God met me there.

Let me share with you three things that proved to me that God was in the corner with me.

First of all, He and I had sweet, sweet fellowship. I wasn't writing back then. I did some journaling, but life was too hectic to have time to set down and write. But I could sing and play the piano. I poured my heart out in song, and the Lord used the lyrics to encourage, comfort, and challenge me. Two songs still sing in my heart from that time in the corner.

One is, He Who Began a Good Work in You. Since Philippians 1:6 is my life's verse, I sang this promise over and over, but there is a bridge lyric that spoke directly to my heart. "If the trouble you're facing is slowly replacing your hope with despair, or the process is long, and you're losing your song in the night. You can be sure that the Lord has His hand on you. Safe and secure, He will never abandon you. You are His treasure, and He finds His pleasure in you."

Oh, my hope was waning, and the process did seem long, but the promise of His continued work gave me the strength to keep going.

The other song was I Choose to Follow. It goes, "I choose to follow, I choose to let you lead. With childlike faith I'll walk each day, knowing that you're all I need. I choose to love you because you've chosen me. Of all the things that I could choose to do, I choose to follow you."

This song burrowed deep into my heart and resolve. As deeply as "Though He slay me, yet will I trust Him," (Job 13:15) had raised me from depression.

I was in a corner, but I had a Friend there beside me. I was not alone. My corner rang with the glories of fellowship.

Another thing that came out of that time home was a chance meeting in a church on the east coast. The conversation happened to move into health, and one woman asked me about mine. I mentioned my pain and difficulty, and she did the most astonishing thing. She purchased a juicer for me and ordered what I called grass and dirt. They were cleansing tablets made from barley and a mix of grains. The dirt was another concoction made up of ground seed hulls, and who knows what – it tasted terrible.

But I put myself on a regime of eating only natural foods, juicing fruits and vegetables, and taking those grass and dirt tablets. I carried on with this for nearly a year. To this day, I no longer suffer from IBS unless I allow my diet to get too full of fake stuff. She saved my life.

And the other thing that came out of my bleak corner was a vision for the future. Toward the end of our furlough, we were in a conference with an older missionary to Australia. His people had prepared his presentation. During this missionary's career, he had seen over 20 churches planted, a Bible College established, and an organized fellowship of pastors.

I sat there listening and encouraged by what God had done through this man's time on the field. Then I heard a whisper in my ear. "Gail, do you believe I could do the same thing in England?" It wasn't Tom whispering – it was the Lord. I took a big gulp and whispered back, "Yes, Lord, I believe you could do that."

That step of believing faith took me out of my corner and placed a renewed and invigorated heart of service within me. I thank the Lord for that hard place; it was another turning point in my life.

Now, some 25 years on, God has precisely done what He challenged me to believe. There is a Bible College with its own premises, a fellowship of pastors, and out of a remarkable ministry through our first church, which alone is a story of God's miraculous direction, God has planted over 20 churches here in England.

Friend, if you are in a hard place, take the hand of the Man standing beside you. Befriend Him as never before. He will teach you about Himself, renew your strength, and give you hope, for He, and only He knows the way out of the corner.

For thought:

What hard place are you facing?
What tough places have you already faced? And how did God work on your behalf?
Can you believe He is with you in the corner today?

Scriptures to consider:

Psalm 23:4, Psalm 25:20, 21, Proverbs 18:10, Philippians 1:6, 1 Peter 5:7

CHOICES

I have a dear friend who shares old books with me. She loves to rummage through bookstores and find the dusty old Christian books, and she has uncovered some incredible jewels.

One writer we enjoy is Marjorie Wilkinson. She published her thoughts back around 1940 and wrote about the war and life in England. Her stories abound with the beautiful old British culture, and her Christian walk is uncomplicated and full of hope. She lets you into her home with a simple candidness that makes you feel like you know her, and you'd love to chat over a cup of tea by her open coal fire.

Well, as I thought over what we might visit about today, I came across a quote I had copied out of one of Marjorie's books called, This One Thing I Know. Her quote comes from a man named Phillip Brooks, an American pastor back in the 1800s. You would know him as the man who penned the lyrics for O Little Town of Bethlehem. How cool is that?

My friend and I often mention how Marjorie wrote for her generation but probably never thought that people some eighty years later would still enjoy and gain from her writing. I believe that is one of the brilliant things about casting bread upon the water. You never know where it will come to shore.

Philip Brooks, too, probably never imagined his lyrics to a simple Christmas hymn would still be being sung over one hundred years later and played over the internet, or that we'd be talking about him today.

Marjorie and Phillip speak of an inward desire to be what God calls them to be. Let me read the quote, and we will talk about it a bit.

He writes, and she shares – "If you give your whole life to loving and serving Christ, one of the blessings of your consecration of yourself to Him will be that in Him there will be open to you a pattern of yourself. You will see your possible self as He sees it, and life will have but one wish and purpose for you, which will be that you may realize that idea of yourself which you have seen in Him."

This quote gets me thinking. If I give my whole life to the love and service of Christ, I will discover more of myself? I will see my possibilities as He sees them, which will motivate me to become what He has shown me? That's what I understand them to be saying.

I know there have been times in my life when the Lord seems to have placed before me a "possible" self – an idea of the future or an intangible goal. A vision clear but obscured, if that makes sense. For a brief moment, I get excited at the possibility, long for the desire, and praise Him for the promise. Then, it slips away, and I face the tasks and hurdles required to reach that vision.

It feels like the Lord dangles a carrot in front of me to keep me going.

What about you? Do you ever get glimpses of what could be? Does God show you things about yourself that match your heart's desires? Even though you can't describe them very well?

It takes me to another of my favorite verses. Psalm 37:4 – "Delight thyself also in the Lord; and he shall give thee the desires of thine heart."

I'm learning that reaching forth is necessary. To take each tiny step by faith with consistency moves me closer to that goal. As I do my part, He will do His. He would not entice me with impossible things, for in Him all things are possible – even those vague visions are His calling to future things in Christ and a deeper level of usefulness and sanctification.

So, what does this mean for us today? I think all of us have hopes and dreams for the future. Ideas of what we would like to do, where we would like to go, and the kind of person we hope we would become through all we are experiencing, but here's the main thing that spoke to my heart through that quote and Psalm 37:4.

I must keep God first. It is easy to wish life away or allow discontent to destroy the image of who Christ wants me to become. I am becoming someone – someone different each day. And so are you.

God is working in our lives to create the person He can use for His glory. We must cooperate with him. To do that, we must love Him and delight in His friendship above all others.

Then, we place ourselves in the position to receive the desires of our hearts. They might be tangible. I know the Lord has reached out and given me many, many things, and I don't discount any of them. I have a wonderful husband, incredible children, and totally perfect grandchildren. I have been allowed to serve the Lord and see Him use me in unexpected ways, but I can't stop there. And neither can you.

God always asks us to continue following. He consistently

works to create the image of Christ in our lives. So, when Marjorie and Phillip talk about a possible self or a pattern of themselves, they are talking about Christ's image imprinted upon their lives. This image, this imprint, became their main desire.

The Apostle Paul puts it this way in Philippians 3:7-10, "But what things were gain to me, those I counted loss for Christ. Yea doubtless, and I count all things but loss for the excellency of the knowledge of Christ Jesus my Lord: for whom I have suffered the loss of all things, and do count them but dung, that I may win Christ, And be found in him, not having mine own righteousness, which is of the law, but that which is through the faith of Christ, the righteousness which is of God by faith: That I may know him, and the power of his resurrection, and the fellowship of his sufferings, being made conformable unto his death."

Dear friend, the world would tell you that such dedication is a waste of your life. But Marjorie and Phillip would disagree.

Let's look beyond today to the person God wants us to be tomorrow. Let's do the next right thing each day, love the Lord with all our heart, soul, and mind, and follow the desires He places with us. We will not be disappointed with our choice.

For thought:

What motivates your Christian life?
Are you drawing closer to finding the image of Christ imprinted on your life?
Do you have a limit to your devotion?
What holds you back?

Scriptures to consider:

Acts 20:24, Ecclesiastes 11:1, 6, Philippians 3:7-10, 13, 14, Romans 12:1,2

THE SCARLET CLOAK

W ould you bear with me to talk about Marjorie again today? I'm going to share a portion from <u>One Thing I Know</u>. The chapter is called *The Scarlet Cloak*. In this chapter, her mother's long illness taught Marjorie to secret herself away in prayer for renewed courage and strength when the burden grew too heavy.

She mentions a poem by Robert Louis Stevenson called The Celestial Surgeon. It goes,

If I have faltered more or less
In my great task of happiness;
If I have moved among my race
And shown no glorious morning face;
If beams from happy human eyes
Have moved me not; if morning skies,
Books, and my food, and summer rain
Knocked on my sullen heart in vain:-
Lord, thy most pointed pleasure take

And stab my spirit broad awake;
Or, Lord, if too obdurate I,
Choose thou, before that spirit die,
A piercing pain, a killing sin,
And to my dead heart run them in!

Obdurate means stubborn or unmoveable. You learn new words when you read old writers.

Marjorie takes the phrase – *my great task of happiness* – in this idea of drawing strength and renewing courage. She knew happiness was not dependent on her circumstances but the position of her heart, a matter of choice. And as a child, this young girl learned to create happiness in the middle of arduous demands. She carried this learning through life, and it shows in her writings.

Marjorie writes, "I realize that to stand up to life, with all my senses fully awake and eager to be used, I need to have my thoughts, feelings, and will rooted in God's will, and to believe wholeheartedly in His plan for my life. When I am apt to forget that I am able to conquer through Christ, the enemies of my peace – fear, ignorance, and inertia in particular – form tangles in my thinking. A sense of guilt emerges from the muddle. Only fresh surrender of my petty self can make way for the larger self that is awaiting life. Then, and then only, will the enemies of destruction, emotionalism, anger, and resentment – be turned into the open sea of usefulness and accomplishment."

Isn't that beautiful? To stand up to the challenges of life (and we face a lot of those, don't we?) Marjorie says we must surrender our petty self and allow the Lord to make us useful and productive.

So, do we do that? Or do we allow the challenges of life to knock us down? Do we have a pity party when things get tough? Does our inertia wane causing us to feel guilty? Do the destructive enemies of peace bring us to our knees in prayer, or do we allow them to rage?

Marjorie goes on to say, "To see your best self – the one

surrendered to God cooperating with Him, taking His resources, working out life together, there must be a "you" loosened from what you might have been and done, reinforced with divine energy and insight, a "you" that does things beyond your capacity, a "you" poised, progressive, productive. But don't look long at this self – look at God. In Him I gaze and grow. In myself I cultivate and deteriorate. I do all things – through Christ which strengthens me."

I love this portion – Have I loosed myself from what I was, and am I now reinforced with divine energy and insight? Do I have faith to attempt things beyond my known capacity? Am I poised, progressive, and productive? Those questions really challenge me.

Then she writes, "With every step forward in the darkness of tomorrow I can claim, as my heritage as a child of God, His presence. Then courage, like a warm scarlet cloak, wraps me about. In faith and growing knowledge of this, I am able, with Him, to feel a tingling sense of a pioneer's adventurous spirit."

Oh, how her writing speaks my heart. Who was she? There isn't much known about her. You can google and find some of her books, but I've not seen a biography. She remains unknown, but her writing speaks volumes.

And how wonderful it is that her words still speak to us today, as they have to others in the past. The march of time from Marjorie's words and other writers of faith shows a translation of devotion and commitment from testimony to testimony, generation to generation, of the Lord's goodness, and His working among His people.

Maybe someday, one hundred years from now, others will draw from our testimonies and our writings. It makes it all so much more important that we tell of God's goodness, that we share our story, for it is His story. As Marjorie puts it, "others have had problems and sorrows and found the way to their solution. I am hand-in-hand with humanity."

Let's wrap ourselves in that Scarlet Cloak of the strength and comfort of Christ and find the happiness, the courage, and fortitude we need to face our world, and let's leave a testimony of His goodness so others can find their way.

For thought:

Who is being influenced by your life?
Do you understand Marjorie's symbol of the Scarlet Cloak?
Are you wrapped in it, and do you know its comfort?
Are you stuck on your creature comforts to the peril of all else?

Scriptures to consider:

2 Corinthians 2:14, 2 Corinthians 4:16-18, 2 Timothy 3:1-5, Philippians 4:9

SHUT THE DOOR

Have you ever used <u>My Utmost for His Highest</u> by Oswald Chambers as your devotional? It is packed with gems, truths, and thoughts that reach out and grab you. His study on Matthew 6:6 caught my attention. The verse reads, "But thou, when thou prayest, enter into thy closet, and when thou hast shut thy door, pray to thy Father which is in secret; and thy Father which seeth in secret shall reward thee openly."

I'll have to share a few quotes from the devotional, so you can see what captured my interest. He writes, "Jesus did not say – "Dream about thy Father in secret but pray to thy Father in secret."

How many times are we guilty of daydreaming and calling it prayer? We tell God what we would like to see happen, we put our ideas before Him and ask Him to bless them, but we aren't looking to see His will. We have settled on our own.

The devotion goes on to say, "After we have entered our secret place and have shut the door, the most difficult thing to do is to pray; we cannot get our minds into working order, and the first thing that conflicts is wandering thoughts. We have to discipline our minds and concentrate on willful prayer."

I got to thinking about this shutting of the door. How often do we go to prayer with all of the burdens, demands, and voices screaming for our attention? We struggle to form a complete prayerful sentence without being distracted. We haven't shut the door! We have brought those things into our secret place, and there isn't room for them and the voice of God. He wants our full attention. I think that's what God is saying when He says, "Shut the door!"

Oswald Chambers puts it this way, "We must have a selected place for prayer and when we get there the plague of flies begins – This must be done, and that. Shut the door. A secret silence means to shut the door deliberately on emotions and remember God."
And it is like a plague of flies, isn't it? We swat one away, and another takes its place. The buzzing creates such a distraction.

We talked about using the drawbridge of our castle to monitor who and what we let into our life. Well, this closet door to our prayer room is very similar. When we go to prayer, we need to shut out the things that distract and interrupt. We have come in secret to talk to our Father who hears in secret, according to Matthew 6:6.

My prayer life has taken several turns throughout my life. As a young teen, I didn't have a regular devotion time. I wasn't taught that. But I did whisper prayers and saw God answer. I knew to get alone to pray, but I really didn't know much more than that.

As a young mother with five children under the age of seven, I went to college, blazed the deputation trail, and went to the mission field before turning 30 years of age. Most of my prayers were grab and run. They were more like cries of desperation and pleas for help. You know the kind. Getting alone for more than thirty seconds was a miracle, and it rarely ever happened.

Then, as life began to take a more measured pace and not demand my antenna up on high, I could take a while to draw aside. I started learning to shut the door. But I found my image of prayer looked much different than what Matthew 6:6 was instructing.

You see, I'm a visual learner. That's why the idea of building walls to aid in depression works so well for me. And when it comes to prayer, I have a visual challenge, too.

As I grew in prayer, I realized I was begging like a suppliant from behind a pillar in the throne room. I was there, but afraid for God to see me. I knew He heard my prayer, and I saw answers, but I found myself hiding, and I had to address it because this is not the image God shows in His word.

I took my little self back to the secret place – to the throne – and ventured new images in my mind.

The first thing I did was step out from behind the pillar. The throne was a long way down the hall, but I learned to open myself to the Lord, not to fear His gaze. From there, I began taking images from God's word and placing myself inside those images within the throne room. I found courage and confidence developed in my prayer life and my walk of faith.

I want to share a few of those images with you today.

We are a child of God, children of the light, the Bible says. What do children do around their father? They sit at His feet. They hold onto His robe or to his hand. They receive a pat on the head or a kindly spoken word. They may even sit in his lap and receive a comforting and reassuring hug. I began approaching my Abba Father in these ways through prayer. I was safer there than anywhere.

There was no need for me to hide behind the pillar when I had a loving Father who wanted only the best for me, who loved me as His child and enjoyed a relationship with me. My prayers took on more connection—an endearing conversation without pressure, a parent/child type of position.

We are a soldier of the cross—sent into a world of need. Just as the disciples came back and reported to Jesus, we report to our commander. We can wrap ourselves in our Scarlet Cloak of the blood of Christ and take our petitions, needs, fears, and challenges to the throne. He will point us to strategies, thwart the enemy, and give us victory. Through Him, we shall do valiantly!

There are so many words of battle used to describe our relationship with the Father. We are to put on the full armor of God, the sword of the Spirit, the helmet of salvation, and arm ourselves to stand against the enemy. Sometimes, prayer looks like a soldier in a flowing robe.

At other times, we are beggars. Like blind Bartimaeus or the woman with the issue of blood, we cannot fix our problem. We enter the throne room on the level of need. Empty of ourselves, helpless and desperate for the King's solution, we fall prostrate before the throne begging for help.

But even here, we are not without promise. Hebrews 4:16 tells us to come boldly unto the throne of grace to find help in time of need. Beggars are welcome! We have come to the right place.

But like Bartimaeus, we need to know what we want. When Jesus stood still, asking what Bartimaeus wanted. He didn't dicker around. "Lord, that I might receive my sight," was his reply.

If we wallow at the throne without knowing why we are there, we are not begging as one in need; we are wallowing in pity. There is a big difference. And the answer from the throne will be different as well. When you come knowing your need, God can answer. When you come to cry and complain, there is no answer because you aren't ready to receive it.

Graciously, we can always come to the throne as a sinner in tears. When we recognize our sinfulness, like Isaiah, we will fall before the throne in humility and brokenness. Or, like Mary, we will know we have been forgiven much, and God uses our tears to cleanse and purify.

I remember the day I came to the throne for forgiveness, expressing my need for a Saviour. God graciously heard and forgave. And, throughout the years, I have had to enter the throne room knowing my guilt and failures, but every time, He has stood and reached out His hand of gracious mercy and welcomed me back.

And there have been times when I was like a lunatic in need of healing. My prayers made no sense. My life was upside down, and my emotions were all over the place, but when I shut that door, the Holy Spirit took over and prayed alongside me. God's healing comfort, His assurance, His understanding, and peace entered my heart, and I left the throne room able to hold things together until the next visit. He put me into my right mind.

Dear friend, it might be time for you to go before the throne, and when you do, remember to shut the door. It is a sacred, intimate place where you go before God Almighty with your requests. And your Father – who seeth in secret – will reward you openly. So, come!

For thought:

Do your prayers sound more like demands or sniveling?
Do you struggle to focus?
What image best describes your prayer life?
Where would you be able to shut the door and have ten minutes alone with your Father?

Scriptures to consider:

Romans 8:15, Hebrews 4:16, Romans 8:26, Psalm 3:1-7, Psalm 63

WHO IS RESTING IN YOUR BOAT?

I do wonder how the future is going to work out. Don't you? With all the unrest, anger, election turmoil, and outright evil going on, and this pandemic with all its uncertainty and chopping and changing, it is enough to rock your boat!

The scripture tells of the disciples out in their boat trying to cross the Sea of Galilee. Everything seemed fine until a 2020 storm blew in. The boat, which seemed so safe, so headed with purpose, and under control, rocked and reeled in the wind. The elements were overtaking them.

Sometimes I feel sorry for these disciples. Their lives and decisions have been on public display for generations. They panicked.

Let's not condemn them too harshly. Some of us have had moments of panic this year. Haven't we? Fear gripped our hearts when everything seemed to be overtaking us and when we felt out of control. I'm sure these guys certainly felt that way.

But down in the belly of the boat lay truth—The Truth. As I got to thinking about this situation, I took heart. There was God – the Son of God – confidently resting. The disciples marveled He could rest during such a storm.

Jesus knew some things they did not know. Things you and I need to know and wholeheartedly believe when we are in a storm and even when our boat is sailing on calmer seas.

That is, we have a God who cannot lie. He will never fail His Word. He will not deceive us or lead us on. So, we can choose to trust and wait. Jesus knew what was going to happen; the disciples did not. God knows what is ahead in 2020 and 2021. We do not, but we can trust Him.

Oswald Chambers says, "Faith must be tested, because it can be turned into a personal possession only through conflict." The disciples were facing such a test. And so are we.

While we are quick to laugh at the disciples' impulsive fears, we should remind ourselves that we often do the same thing. Instead of calmly trusting and waiting on the Lord, we rush into prayer with an irrational urgency.

Chambers went on to say, "Faith is unutterable trust in God, trust which never dreams that He will not stand by us."

Here is where I always think the disciples weren't maybe as irrational as we like to paint them. They knew Who was in the boat with them, and they had come to the right place for help—to their Saviour. Jesus talks to them about fear and little faith, and that brings another thought.

Fear often walks alongside faith. It is the challenge, the difficulty; it is fear that presses the issue of faith. It is the test that develops strength for deeper waters and further adventures. Each time we face a test of our faith, we will see the hand of God, the presence of the Saviour, and the comfort of the Spirit.

Have you not found that true in your life? I know I have.

Missionary Amy Carmichael experienced an extended period of ill health. During that time, she wrote a book entitled <u>Rose from Brier</u>. As I read the chapter, <u>All Is Well</u>; she, too, began talking about storms.

You know, there may be more storms ahead of us. We aren't on the other side of the sea yet. There is no promise of a calm passage. Amy says, "Let us settle it, therefore, in our hearts, as something that cannot be shaken, that our first prayer, our deepest desire, shall not be for blue skies and sweet airs, but that we may always have the ungrieved presence of the Captain and the Master in our ship."

As we work our way toward the ending of 2020, let's remember Who is resting in our boat. All is well if His presence is there. Let's not allow any fear or temptation to keep us from resting assuredly in His love come fair weather or foul.

If there are more surprises ahead, more stormy waters, more fearful winds, let's remember that there is enough grace for each day. We need not fear failing before the end of the journey, for He is our assurance. He will take us through. He will give us grace to endure and to conquer in the moment of need—day by day.

Amy closes her chapter with a prayer. "O Saviour…hast Thou ever failed the soul that trusted Thee? Never, never," She says, "By the merits of Thy Blood, all is well, all shall be well."

Amen. All is well. Today is safe and secure. Live it in faith, thankfulness, and the joy of His abiding presence. All shall be well – it has been so in the past, through dark the skies and rough the waters. And it shall be so in the future---He has promised. Our future is secured. He goes before us. We can ride the storm by faith in God who cannot lie and, notwithstanding, no matter what comes, He stands by us. He rests in our boat. May we keep silence before Him until we come to shore.

For thought:

When have you panicked or experienced fear in 2020?
Do you know the abiding presence of God in your life?
Who is resting in your boat?

Scriptures to consider:

Mark 4:39, Titus 1:2, 2 Corinthians 12:9, 2 Timothy 4:17, Hebrews 11:6

THE MENDING BASKET

My mother had two baskets, an ironing basket, and a mending basket. You know what those are, but very few of us have them anymore. Our tumble dryers and fabrics mean ironing is becoming a thing of the past, and as far as mending goes, not many people know how to darn socks or put on a button, much less replace a zipper.

But years ago, mending kept the family clothed. People weren't able to afford a new pair of trousers every month, and if you outgrew your skirt, you would just let it out a bit. Or take it in if you were lucky enough to lose weight.

This idea of mending came to me from a little book I was reading called, <u>Within My Home</u> by Eleanor Vellacott Wood. Again, it's an old book. She tells the story of a weary woman mending with a needle and thread. Once done, she took her aching back and fingers to bed. As was her custom, she paused to read before finishing her day and came to a Scripture that set her mind thinking.

The scripture is 1 Peter 5:10. The King James reads, "But the God of all grace, who hath called us unto his eternal glory by Christ Jesus, after that ye have suffered a while, make you perfect, stablish, strengthen, settle you."

The woman in the story read from the Moffatt translation, which uses these three words: repair, recruit, and strengthen. The word repair caught her attention.

She had been doing just that all evening – repairing and mending.

So today, let's visit a bit about mending. To mend means to fix back together, to restore, or to repair.

Peter, who penned those words in 1 Peter 5:10, knew about mending because he often mended his nets on the shores of Galilee. That's also what James and John were doing when Jesus called them. These men knew the patience it took to piece together broken ends. And when Peter denied the Lord, he knew what it meant to need mending for himself.

In Ezekiel 34:16, God says, "I will seek that which was lost, and bring again that which was driven away, and will bind up that which was broken, and will strengthen that which was sick." That's what Jesus did for Peter. Remember? "Simon, son of Jonas, lovest thou me," Jesus restored Peter – he mended him.

How many times have we felt broken? Have we experienced ugly gashes in our lives that only the Master's hand can repair? Have we lost our temper, been harassed by things left undone, and failed to express patience and care? There are many, many breaks in our nets, far too many to list, and they need an expert Mender? Jesus is the Divine Mender.

Friend, we must fall on our knees and ask the Lord to mend the break of sin in our life in the matter of salvation and sanctification. We need His Mending Hands to touch us, to bind up our wounds as we read in Psalm 147:3, and to heal our broken hearts. No other hands mend like His.

The author writes, "They (Jesus' hands) were pierced by the nails of Calvary, and three days later they burst the bonds of death, in order that they might mend this cruel break. Wondrous, triumphant Mender! Nothing is beyond His power. The break of sin in your life may have been grievous. But the God of all Grace WILL repair you!" This is the gospel story.

Our mending was costly. Jesus paid the bitter price of denial, the traitorous betrayal, and gave his own life to make us whole. Yet how gently and patiently He touches our wounded places caused by our sin and self-will. He gives back the wasted years and forgives our mistakes. He restores us to usefulness.

And what does He call us to do? We are to be menders as well. To bear burdens, to speak the truth in love, to warn and encourage those around us. Look at this list from Isaiah 58:6, 7. He calls his children to:

Loose the bands of wickedness,
To undo the heavy burdens,
To let the oppressed go free,
To break every yoke,
To deal bread to the hungry,
To bring the poor to their houses,
And to make garments for those without clothing.

The author writes, "Homely work this! within the power of every woman. It is possible," she writes, "that someone might write her name against at least one item on this list, and in doing so, might volunteer for some special bit of mending work. Isaiah 58:12 says, "Thou shall be called, the repairer of the breach."

It is a blessed thing to know the Lord can and will repair us. We need our holes mended, our wounds bound up, and our broken hearts healed by the Master, but if we take these blessings without giving in return, we are unprofitable and unthankful servants.

Today, look to see who needs your mending hand. Who might the Lord have placed in your basket? Who might need your help to break free from wickedness, to carry a heavy burden, to have enough food to eat, to heat their home, or even a new coat for their back or shoes for their children?

God wants to use us to mend others. Are we willing? I hope so. There are many hurting and broken people out there. More of us need to get out our needle and thread and weave some loving strength back into our homes, communities, and churches.

Then, we can be known as someone who repairs the breaches.

For thought:

Where do your nets need mending?
Have you experienced repair from the Divine Mender?
What part of the service of mending from Isaiah 58:6,7 might you undertake to help others and become a repairer of the breach?

Scriptures to consider:

1 Peter 5:10, Psalm 147:3, Isaiah 58:6,7, Galatians 5:13, Galatians 6:2

WE ARE NOT DESOLATE

We have visited about contentment, breathing in the right atmosphere, keeping ourselves in the love of God, feeling exhausted, and needing a good cry. We talked about being stuck in a corner and how to wrap ourselves in that Scarlet Cloak. We looked at staying dedicated and shutting the door so our prayer life is more powerful. We reminded ourselves that our Lord is in the boat with us and that He is the mender of our lives who calls us to participate with Him in mending others.

Today, let's visit Psalm 34. It isn't a long psalm, only 22 verses, but packed with thoughts, assurances, and more of the precious promises of God. Last year I memorized this Psalm. I don't know if I could repeat it word for word today, but God still brings phrases of it to mind that have helped me these past months.

It starts with verse one, "I will bless the Lord at all times: his praise shall continually be in my mouth."

At all times, continually – are we blessing and praising the Lord to this extent? It's quite a challenge, isn't it? If we are at all times, continually blessing and praising, it leaves little time for moaning and complaining.

Verses two and three, "My soul shall make her boast in the Lord; the humble shall hear thereof, and be glad. O magnify the Lord with me, and let us exalt his name together."

We encourage each other when we share what God is doing. Have you shared a recent blessing with someone else? Given them the word of your testimony? Have you boasted about God's goodness? He's a delightful topic of conversation.

Verse four, "I sought the Lord, and he heard me, and delivered me from all my fears."

All my fears. We had lots of those this year, didn't we? But God calms our hearts and delivers us from all of them when we call on Him!

Verse five, "They looked unto him, and were lightened; and their faces were not ashamed."

We find confidence when we look to the Lord for our help. And that confidence is like a beam on our face; others see Jesus. Oh, how the world needs to see Him.

Verse six, "This poor man cried, and the Lord heard him, and saved him out of all his troubles."

All his troubles – every one of them. We only have to cry out for His help. We can't fix it by ourselves. Only he can save us, and he will – from every trouble.

Verse seven, "The angel of the Lord encampeth round about them that fear him, and delivereth them."

God's angels are all around us. Like Elijah's servant, we need eyes to see. God is ready to deliver. The sound of the trumpet grows nearer every day.

Verses eight to ten, "O taste and see that the Lord is good: blessed is the man that trusteth in him. O fear the Lord, ye his saints: for there is no want to them that fear him. The young lions do lack, and suffer hunger; but they that seek the Lord shall not want any good thing."

Wow! God will meet my needs. I will not lack anything. He is that good to me.

Verses eleven and twelve, "Come, ye children, hearken unto me: I will teach you the fear of the Lord. What man is he that desireth life, and loveth many days, that he may see good?"

Do you want to have a good life? Then learn to fear the Lord and do this – Verses twelve to fourteen, "Keep thy tongue from evil, and thy lips from speaking guile. Depart from evil, and do good; seek peace, and pursue it."

Why? Because, verses fifteen to seventeen say, "The eyes of the Lord are upon the righteous, and his ears are open unto their cry. The face of the Lord is against them that do evil, to cut off the remembrance of them from the earth. The righteous cry and the Lord heareth, and delivereth them out of all their troubles."

There is it again – deliverance from all their troubles for those who trust the Lord.

Verse eighteen, "The Lord is nigh unto them that are of a broken heart; and saveth such as be of a contrite spirit."

Here is the difference between the righteous and the evil. The righteous have a broken heart and a repentant spirit; they seek peace and pursue. The wicked do not!

Verses nineteen and twenty, "Many are the afflictions of the righteous: but the Lord delivereth him out of them all. He keepeth all his bones; not one of them is broken."

All! What a wonderful word – a great promise! The Lord delivereth him out of them all! Do you need an answer to your affliction? Ask the Lord. Claim this promise. He will keep His word.

Verse twenty-one, "Evil shall slay the wicked; and they that hate the righteous shall be desolate."

The law of sowing and reaping does not change. The wicked get caught in their own trap.

And here's the verse that makes my heart sing.

Verse twenty-two, "The Lord redeemeth the soul of his servants; and none of them that trust in him shall be desolate."

None of them that trust in him shall be desolate. What does desolate mean? You have to put the two phrases of this verse together. The first phrase promises redemption – The Lord redeemeth (buys back) the soul of his servants. And the second phrase could read, none of them that place their trust in the Lord will be held guilty. They are released from bondage, redeemed from slavery, and saved eternally.

I like the way Matthew Henry describes this verse. "The Lord redeems the soul of his servants from the power of the grave and from the sting of every affliction. He keeps them from sinning in their troubles, which is the only thing that would do them a mischief, and keeps them from despair, and from being put out of the possession of their own souls. None of those that trust in him shall be desolate, that is, they shall not be comfortless, for they shall not be cut off from their communion with God. No man is desolate but he whom God has forsaken, nor is any man undone till he is in hell. Those that are God's faithful servants, that make it their care to please him and their business to honour him, and in doing so trust him to protect and reward them, and, with good thoughts of him, refer themselves to him, have reason to be easy whatever befalls them, for they are safe and shall be happy."

None of them—none of us— that put our trust in Him shall be desolate.

Dear friend, we are not desolate, without comfort or hope. The angels of our Father surround us, ready to deliver. The ear of God attends our prayers, and He promises deliverance from all afflictions if we will but cry out to Him.

Is it any wonder then that the first verses hold such a precious instruction? "I will bless the Lord at all times; his praise shall be continually in my mouth! O magnify the Lord with me, and let us exalt his name together."

For thought:

What words are continually coming from your mouth?
Are you aware of the angels encamped all around you?
Honestly, do you lack any good thing?
Do you actively seek peace in your life?

Scriptures to consider:

Philippians 2:14, James 3:13-18, 1 Peter 3:8-12, Psalm 40:17

Made in the USA
Columbia, SC
22 June 2022